Didi

The Life and Death of a Hidden Artist

AMY MCELHOSE

WestBow Press books may be ordered through booksellers or by contacting:

WestBow Press
A Division of Thomas Nelson & Zondervan
1663 Liberty Drive
Bloomington, IN 47403
www.westbowpress.com
1 (866) 928-1240

ISBN: 978-1-9736-9481-6 (sc)
ISBN: 978-1-9736-9483-0 (hc)
ISBN: 978-1-9736-9482-3 (e)

Library of Congress Control Number: 2020911764

Print information available on the last page.

WestBow Press rev. date: 04/13/2022

WESTBOW
P R E S S®
A DIVISION OF THOMAS NELSON
& ZONDERVAN

Thank you to my husband for helping me find the words, for holding me up when I needed to fall, and for always being the best part of my life. And thank you, God, for never giving up on me.

Mom taught me that as a girl I could be and do anything I wanted—
she was right.

Introduction

The odds are pretty high you didn't know my mom. I mean, how could you have? She rarely left the house. Those who did know her though were blessed to meet such a special lady.

For those who didn't know her, my mom was born and raised in Charleston, South Carolina. The middle child of her family, she grew up with three sisters and a younger brother in a household most would define as poor. Even though wealth or status never defined her, I know her upbringing made her who she was.

She met my father, who was serving in the navy at the time, when she was nineteen and married him not long after her twentieth birthday. Michael, my oldest brother, was born after Mom and Dad had only been together a year. After many failed attempts, and another five years, I came along. About a year after me, my youngest brother, Andrew, was born and completed our family.

We were a pretty average family, to me at least. What I did notice was that throughout my childhood, Mom found more and more reasons not to leave the house. It became even more apparent to me once my brothers and I were out of school. It was never clinically diagnosed, but I know she was agoraphobic. Mom instead created her own world right in our home. In her world, she found happiness and comfort far greater than being out in public could ever offer to her. For all the years I can remember, she filled her time at home creating conventional art and everything in between.

Growing up, I was my mom's shadow. If she was in a chair, I was right next to her. She was my everything. Looking back on my progression to adulthood, I know that she instilled many of the values I hold dearly to my heart. Life was abundant with art, music, and God because I was her daughter.

Like my mom, I was twenty when I got married. When that relationship fell apart seven years later, my mom was there to pick me up after I had fallen and helped take care of my newborn son. She was my rock, and I really couldn't ever fathom her not being around. I guess you could call it denial on my part. My mom was a heavy smoker, ate whatever made her happy, and rarely went to the doctor. Not exactly the recipe for a long, healthy life.

It amazes me how fast the years came and went. I remarried, gained a stepson, and eventually, had a daughter of my own. My relationship with my mom gradually evolved because she realized I had my own life that demanded me. I still made it a point to visit her every week, but looking back, I wish I could have spent every free moment with her. That's the funny thing about death. It makes you second-guess all the choices you made, however inconsequential they seem.

When Mom died, it was all I could think about at first. Every moment of every breath reminded me of her. A smell, a song, and of course the memories that would follow. She would look back at me in the mirror when I was putting on my makeup, and she is still the first person I think of when I have good news to share. After almost three months, every day seems to get a little better—perhaps more distant from the harsh reality. I can go for a lot of the day and not think much about missing her—well, until I do. Some days that feels like a ton of bricks on my soul, and other days it feels like a little memory that is nice to visit for a while. Mostly, I sink into both, at different times of the day. People say things will get easier; I just can't imagine.

Selfishly, this book is therapeutic for me, but that wasn't my reason for writing it. I never knew about the process involved in having to let someone go whom you love so dearly. It certainly wasn't obvious to me because it seemed like no one ever talked about it. My hope is that sharing Mom's story can provide a perspective that you may not have heard before. At the same time, I want to showcase some of the art that was my mom's passion for all these years. The art she made was far more than I could ever have printed in a single book, but a collection of her last works adorns the pages of this one, along with the story of her final days on this earth.

Welcome to the story of my mom, Didi, as the grandkids called her.

Tuesday

You never know what a day holds when you wake up.

Being a part-time banker, my days off vary from week to week. I was looking forward to Tuesday and for the visit with my mom that I had promised her. When I arrived at my parents' house, I was surprised to find no one home. I ran through the possibilities in my head and concluded that maybe Mom and Dad had gone to the doctor's since Mom hadn't been feeling the best. It had just been Friday that she had received the results of a CT scan the doctor had ordered—a mass was found in her lungs. Her head had been hurting badly too, but the MRI was scheduled much farther out than what we had hoped for—another two weeks. A quick call to Dad's cell phone resulted in leaving a voice mail and deciding to wait around a bit. After a good thirty minutes, I made the choice to head home and started my forty-minute drive back.

I was relieved when the phone rang to see it was my father calling me back. Dad told me that the doctor had advised Mom to go to the hospital since they could immediately do testing to diagnose why her head was hurting. Also, he was hoping to better determine what the mass was in her chest. Dad assured me that everything was fine, that Mom was in good hands, and that he would call me later to let me know what, if anything, had been found out.

By the time my father called again, it was evening. The hospital was admitting Mom to complete all the tests that they felt were necessary. Knowing I had the next day off too, I volunteered to come to the hospital as soon as I had gotten my daughter, Caitlyn, on the bus for school in the morning. We said our goodbyes, and I felt a little peace for the moment. Mom had been complaining of her head hurting for a while but had procrastinated about seeing the doctor for it. I was happy she was finally somewhere getting help.

Didi loved nature which can
be seen in her artwork

Wednesday

Don't take a day for granted; ask all your questions now.

Carrying my crochet bag along with me, I entered the hospital and located my mom's room on the sixth floor. When I entered her room, she was watching Animal Planet, one of her favorite things to do. I was content to sit with her and crochet. Dad had gone back to the house to let the dogs out, so it was just her and me. The conversation was typical, and it wasn't that of someone who was worried. In retrospect, I wish I had the foresight to ask all the questions I had always wanted to know the answers to. I didn't realize the opportunity was about to pass me by.

When the pulmonologist entered the room, we spoke to him together. Mom's mind wasn't as sharp as it once was, and simple details would often lapse her memory. She told me that she preferred me to be there to listen and remember, then we would be able to discuss the details later. The doctor advised us that he would like to biopsy the mass in her lungs to verify that it was cancer. By determining its type, they would know how to better treat it. Following protocol, he warned us of the risk of performing a surgery of any type and then joked, "I haven't lost a patient performing this surgery." Having faith in the doctor, my mom responded, "Whatever you think. You are the doctor. I'm going to listen to you."

The doctor's response was "It is your final decision because it is your body."

Listening intently, I could easily hear the business side of this conversation. He needed to get her consent to perform the surgery, and my mom thought she wouldn't be asked to do the surgery if it wasn't deemed necessary.

What wasn't discussed was what the real benefit of the diagnostic test was and whether it would even have a positive effect. If they determine the type of cancer, would she want to treat it anyway? What were the usual treatments for similar cases? Was the test worth the risk? Had anyone asked her these questions when I wasn't there? Of course these questions all came in hindsight. It's twenty-twenty, after all.

I imagine this may have been her dream: a log cabin in the woods, a fire burning in the fireplace, birds singing, and the smell of coffee permeating the space. All you can craft surrounds your fingertips; you just have to walk outside.

Day 3

Thursday

You only get one chance—no do-overs.

I called out of work to be with Mom because she asked me to be there. It was about 10:00 a.m. when they came and took her for surgery. I had prepared myself for the day with a homemade lunch and more crocheting to pass the time, while I waited in the room for her return. The oncologist and the pulmonologist stopped by and saw me to discuss some additional details. This was reassuring since it was the first time that I had been able to speak with the cancer doctor directly. He knowledgeably answered my questions, so I felt I had a much better idea of what the potential outcomes were.

After the surgery had been completed, the pulmonologist came in and warned that the "patient" needed a little more recovery time. He said that Mom had some difficulties during the surgery and now they wanted her to come through recovery slower so that no additional problems were created when they withdrew the scope from her lungs. Just as I acknowledged the news, Dad arrived back to relieve me so that I could go home and get my youngest off the bus.

When I got back home and settled, I phoned my dad to check on things. Dad told me that Mom was brought back around five and was resting comfortably in her room. I told him I would call back later when Mom was awake so I could talk to her. Since I had spent my day at the hospital, I hadn't had the chance to think about dinner, so my family and I went out. While waiting for the table to become available, I called Mom to see how she was feeling. Her throat was sore from the surgery, so I offered to bring her some pudding and Jell-O. She had not been eating much, and I thought food may make her feel a little better and that the coolness could help soothe her throat. She liked that idea.

Not long after I hung up, I realized that I couldn't quite make it back to the hospital in time to be within the visiting-hour guidelines. I decided to call the nurses' station to verify how strict their policy was, and they confirmed that the cutoff was 8:00 p.m. The nurse, understanding my concern, happily agreed to comply with my food promise. I called Mom back to let her know about the situation and told her I was sorry that I couldn't make it back in time. She said she was sorry too, and I could easily hear it in her voice.

Had I known what the next day would hold, I would have broken any and all the rules to see her that night. You only get one chance—no do-overs.

Day 4

Friday

Write all you can; write so the words don't escape you.

My sleep was sporadic that night. Around 3:00 a.m., I woke. I was excited and worried about what the day ahead held and eager for it to begin. My dreams had been filled that night with thoughts of Mom, so all I could think about was her when I opened my eyes. Did the Jell-O help her throat? Was she hungry? Did the nurse find the pudding last night?

I had to work at ten, so I planned to visit with her for as long as possible until then. Knowing that my father might not spend all day at the hospital, I had decided that I didn't want Mom to be lonely or feel bored without any of us there. In turn, I downloaded some gospel and country music, her favorites, on my computer and compiled a playlist titled "Mom" to ensure she wouldn't get confused with any of my other music. I was also concerned that she wasn't getting enough nutrition, so I made her a peanut butter and jelly sandwich and cut up some fresh fruit to take to her. *Some of her old-time favorites should spark her appetite*, I thought. Everything was packed into my car, and as soon as I had gotten my daughter on the bus, I was off to the hospital.

When I arrived at my mom's room and opened the door, to my surprise, she wasn't there. There sat before me a completely different woman who was about Mom's age, graying hair on the edges, and placed exactly where I'd left my mother. I was confused and leaned back to verify the room number on the door. Sure enough, it was the correct room. It seemed like this woman was as shocked as me, so I apologized, shut the door, and headed straight to the nurses' station. Many thoughts began swirling in my head. *Did they switch rooms? Did they send her home? Why wasn't I told?*

At the nurses' station, there was a brief discussion between the nurses until a quick agreement was reached about who was going to help me. A very polite nurse said, "Let me take you to where she was moved last night." Our journey back out to the hallway and into the elevator seemed like forever. The nurse explained, "Last night your mom had some trouble catching her breath. We tried switching her from slow-flow oxygen to high-flow and she was still unable to catch her breath."

I had to catch my breath. What was she telling me?

The nurse continued. "We called your father, and he gave consent to insert a breathing tube because she just wasn't able to breathe."

The door off the elevator was one where the nurse must wave her badge to get it to open, and slowly it opened. We took a wrong turn down a hallway and the nurse quickly found her bearing and redirected us. She began telling me more about the circumstances, but all I heard were the footsteps on the ground as we walked. *Is she alive?* I think.

Just then, a wave of her badge opened another door. This was the ICU door. Fear rushed over me as we made our way to the round desk at the opening of the unit. Here, all I could see were symmetrical rooms lined with patients who didn't seem to be doing very well. The occupants of each seemed like they had a plethora of different problems. Some rooms had nurses or a doctor or two that were milling about; others had just a patient. Things seemed very silent here, apart from the beeping of machines and monitors.

She led me to another nurse who was charged with escorting me the rest of the way. The first nurse apologized for the situation, and I was turned over to the round desk nurse who proceeded to tell me about the condition of my mother. A feeling of loneliness overwhelmed me. The bag of goodies I brought was in one hand, and my purse, crochet bag, and her music entertainment were in the other. This was obviously not how I expected the morning to go. She instructed me to put on a gown and to wear rubber gloves at all times.

Finally, I was with my mom in her "new" room.

The room was weakly lit, and she had a big tube coming out of her throat, which seemed to take up the entire center of the room. Behind her was a monitor with sharp waves on the screen. I approached her and immediately went to her side. There were more wires and tubes coming from her arm than I had initially realized and even more tubes feeding into her mouth. On the monitor above, I saw her blood pressure, heart rate, and blood oxygen levels. A small machine that the IV and feeding tubes were connected to sat to her right. I would soon learn that it was supplying morphine in addition to fluids.

I found an open spot on her hand that I could hold and meekly said, "Hi, Momma."

Her eyes, which had been closed, opened as she heard my voice. This seemed good.

Seeing my mom lying in disarray was heartbreaking. It took all my energy and strength to not break down and burst into tears, but I didn't want her to worry.

Her eyes opened and closed a few times before she seemed to wake up enough to be coherent. I told her "I'm so sorry you're here, Mom." As the words came out, a feeling of sadness overcame me as I fought back tears. But some slipped through. A look of worry was washed on her face, and feeling bad, I tried to shield my eyes by hanging my head down so she couldn't see my eyes.

She heard my voice though, and her eyes widened as if she was questioning her mortality. The nurse, being quick on her feet and having done this many times before, chimed in with "Your daughter is just worried about you and wants you to know she loves you very much."

She was right. It was just enough to remind me that I had to regain my composure and get myself together for her. I don't remember all the words that came next, but I know I told her I love her.

My dad showed up just as the floor shift change occurred. I briefly stepped outside of the room to call my husband, Craig, and fill him in on the unexpected events. He was close by and offered to come to the hospital to be with Dad and me. This seemed like a great idea, and I immediately accepted his offer. I already knew that I would desperately need his support to help get me through this day. Next, I called my boss to tell him about my mom. He was so supportive and told me to take the time I need. He must have heard the shaking in my voice.

Time seemed to pass slowly until his arrival. I felt broken, like someone had clipped my imaginary wings and the realness of the situation was weighing me down. When Craig got there, I filled him in on the rules and then helped him into a gown and some gloves. He made his way to Mom's bedside and held her hand. She couldn't talk because of the tube, but she could gesture with her eyes and hands. Mom had been through a lot the night prior, and it showed in her energy level; she seemed wiped.

The nurse suggested that we give Mom a piece of paper to see if she felt up to writing in lieu of talking. My father, Craig, and I talked across her bed, and she seemed to enjoy just hearing us talk. In fact, she had even gestured to keep talking, like she gained comfort from it. We did.

It wasn't long after offering the paper that she wrote some words. As my husband told her that he loved her, she wrote her response. "I love you too."

After this, our conversation turned to a multitude of topics about things like my cat not being nice to my houseplants. Mom grabbed the pencil and wrote, "Moth balls." Craig asked if she meant moth balls to repel the cat from the plant, and she mildly shook her head yes. We laughed at the fact that Mom was trying to help even when she was in this difficult situation.

Dad chimed in, "No, Shirley, it's not your time yet," with tears in his eyes.

It is those moments that matter. Inside, you are breaking apart and you are writhing in pain, but outside, you must show a face of strength, resilience, and most importantly, confidence. All of this so she will believe too.

The next words spilled from my mouth. "No, Momma, we just have to wait until you can get off of this machine. Last night when you couldn't breathe, they had to intubate you."

For us, the goal was simple: get her off that machine and just bring her back home. Unfortunately, we knew even that was just an interim to death. Her body was giving up, and the machine had just forced us to see that fact.

It occurred to me, after that moment, that the irony of the situation is what you want for your mom the most is to believe what you know isn't true. Throughout my life, it was always her place to reassure, give confidence in bad situations, and offer hugs to make everything all better. In this situation, the tables had turned and now it was my task.

It was that first day in ICU, knowing things were not good, I thought, *You were here for my first breath, and I'll be here for your last.*

$\mathcal{D}ay$ 5

Saturday

Bring your family together as much as possible. Tomorrow may be too late.

The weekend had come much faster than I expected, and at first, that Saturday was starting much like any other. The main difference was the early morning frenzy of getting the kids up and ready to go to my in-laws' house. Normally, Saturdays would entail a short workday for me, while Craig and the kids would have a low-key morning watching their favorite shows together. This one was noticeably different though, as we began our drive to Craig's parents' house.

After dropping off the kids, we arrived at the hospital, which was close by. Mom's room was greatly unchanged. The view out the window to the hallway had the same sign on the wall from the prior day. "You can't have a CAUTI if you don't have a FOLEY." We had joked about this throughout the first day, thinking it was odd sounding. We even went so far as to ask the doctors what it meant. They explained, "Catheter-associated UTI is the CAUTI, and FOLEY was the name for the gentleman who had made the catheter." It's funny how these small details that seemed to mean nothing are the ones to stand out the most. Still hooked up to machines, there lay my mom.

Nurses had been coming in often to adjust settings, refill an IV, or notate her vitals. Incredibly, they always maintained a high level of professionalism and decorum while they worked. Not an easy job, to say the least. They even had to slide Mom back up in the bed as she would gradually slide down with gravity as time wore on. Of course, the effort took a couple of nurses. It was a helpless feeling as I watched them lower the bed so that she was flat on her back. Her body didn't seem to like it. The nurses positioned themselves on each side of Mom as they grabbed the padding that was placed underneath of her. In almost a coordinated way, they pulled up toward the top of the bed. "One, two, three," they counted off. And in unison, they pulled toward the top of the bed. Once she was better situated, they rocked her to one side to get the padding out from underneath her weight to replace it. As they put her to what seemed like an extreme position on her side, she was almost face-first on the bed. I whispered to her, "They are almost done, Momma. Just changing your padding to make you more comfortable."

Being just a spectator, I felt her embarrassment of not being able to do it for herself and the breathlessness as she is tossed to her side.

had been maintaining my "guard" position until my hand went numb from squeezing my mom's hand too tight. Then a nurse asked me to shift to the other side while they emptied the condensation from a tube. "The condensation builds up because they put moisture in the air to keep her airways from drying out," the nurse explained to me.

After she left, I became acutely aware of the water collecting in the line's lowest point and worried that she would aspirate and bring fluid into her lungs. It was strange to feel so scared for her and helpless at the same time. My only power was to ask the nurse about it, and she told me not to worry and drained the tube. I was worried and, for the first time in my life, not in control. I was really scared.

I prayed to ask for the only hope I could find. "Please, God, bring my mom from this." I have begged this in my mind. Could he answer it now?

Mom seemed more sedated that morning. She wasn't doing any writing anymore, and our window of opportunity was gone for communication with written words. What we did have were occasional hand squeezes and eye movements that we would exchange. I've heard that communication is 90 percent nonverbal and we found out how true that statement really is. We noticed this more and more throughout the day and were just as easily frustrated by it too.

My phone rang out in the hallway and I hurried to grab it. It was out of the room in my purse because we were in a clean environment and our belongings were to be kept outside of the room. When I saw the name "Michael" on the caller ID, I answered the phone. I was struggling to get the gloves off so that my hands could air out while I talked. The automated operator on the phone asked me to pick the selection to talk with the inmate. Michael has been in jail for a few months but called every week or so. He had heard the news of Mom being in the ICU from Dad, so he tried to call on Friday, but I missed his call.

"Hi, Amy," he said.

He sounded so somber and far away. Part of his voice sounded relieved that he got in touch with me, and the other part worried for Mom.

I updated him on how the morning was going and advised that nothing much had changed. I put him on speaker so I could bring the phone to Mom's bedside so she could hear his voice. Michael started with "Hi Mom. I love you." And we asked her, "Do you hear Michael? He's on the phone for you."

At that exact moment, she squeezed Craig's hand in acknowledgment. She was hearing him even through the sedation!

Craig said, "She squeezed my hand! She hears you!"

Mike said it again. "I love you, Mom! You need to get better so you can be home when I get there. You are gonna get better. Just get rest and let your body heal."

She squeezed Craig's hand again, and we were happy that we knew she was hearing Mike's voice.

We all took turns talking to him so Mom could listen to our conversations. I can't really remember now what we said or talked about, but it felt good to have him there, even if only on the phone in a limited capacity. I very much needed my big brother's guidance, positive thoughts, and strength.

His call was limited to thirty minutes and the time was nearing its end, so he said his goodbyes to her. Although he didn't realize it, this would be the very last time he got to tell Mom that he loved her.

Knowing the call was coming to an end, we gave our love to him, but before hanging up, he offered up a few words of brotherly advice. "Just keep telling her that she is going to get better so she can go home." He ended with "Stay positive, Amy. You have to be there for us and be strong for Mom. I know you can do it."

I told him to call me later so I could fill him in on any changes and then the call ends.

Barely a few minutes had passed, and I heard my phone ring again. This time Andrew's name was showing on the caller ID as I answered.

My younger brother's voice was a welcomed sound. After filling him in on the events of the morning, I put him on speaker. "Hi, Mom," he said in his gruff, manly voice.

This time it was Dad who said, "She hears you, Andrew," as he felt Mom squeeze his hand.

Andrew responded, "I love you, Mom! As soon as you get off that machine, you will be able to go home."

It was clear he didn't really know what to say next, but who would?

A few minutes later, he too was saying his final words to her. "Goodbye, Mom. You get better soon, and I'll talk to you then. I love you, Mom."

His voice was seeming less confident and shakier than when I had answered the phone, but it was obvious Mom understood everything. And once again, she squeezed a hand in acknowledgment.

When the doctor came back into the room, he began to look at the screens intently. I was sitting on the other side of my mom when he said, "She is struggling to stay in sync with the machine."

His words took a solid form in my imagination as I tried to define what that really meant for Mom. My quick synopsis: she was using the machine to breathe, and she was battling with controlling the machine. *Just like Mom to be so stubborn,* I think. But this sync was life and death. How do we achieve sync? When do we know it is working? How do we make her understand what she needs to do?

I stood up as our conversation continued across Mom's bed. Mom might like this since she always seemed to like to be a part of these types of conversations. My questions and his answers followed, but what caught my attention was that as the doctor and I stood there talking, she looked prideful. Across her face was a half-cocked smile with the right of her mouth drawn back, kind of like a smirk with less attitude, and her eyes were closed as if she was listening. This was what she wanted me here for: she knew that I wasn't afraid to talk to the doctors. In fact, she knew that I would ask every question I could think to ask, and when those ran out, I'd find more.

In that moment, I had solace knowing that I was doing everything she wanted. It became apparent to me that the doctor defined sync as a diagnostic process. I was initially viewing it as a verb or an action and something concrete that you can do (or not do in this case). The doctor told me that to help her achieve this, they would increase her pain medication to keep her relaxed and not fight the machine. In my mind, I was thinking about willingness to live and mind over matter mentality, so I said out loud with my eyes squinting in thought, "But isn't that a good thing, her trying to breathe on her own?"

He tried to better convey and define his strategy by offering more technical information, which was lost on me at that moment.

Shortly after the doctor left the room, Dad expressed his need to leave and do necessary home chores and stood up to exit. He made his way to Mom to kiss her on her forehead in the familiar way he had so many times over for the last forty-eight years.

While holding her hand, he whispered to her that he loved her. Showing his heartfelt playfulness for her, he then jokingly said, "Now try and breathe in sync with that machine while I'm gone." He offered a little giggle and a finger poke to the air as if to imply she needed to do better, technically.

In pure momma fashion, she lifted her hand and offered him her own choice finger on her right hand. Of course, we all laughed and thought it was nice to see her personality still coming through, even in these conditions. He dashed back to her side to offer a last kiss on the head and then hurried out the door.

Once again alone with Mom, Craig and I stood on either side of her bed while talking to each other and every so often saying something reassuring to her. She started to lift her hand and banged it against the mattress as if she was frustrated. I tried desperately to read her eyes and understand her needs. Over the years, there were many times I could glance at her and instantly, as if reading her mind, know what she was thinking or feeling. This time though, it was different. I didn't know, so we tried to soothe her. "Mom, we will take you home. We just need you off of this machine."

Down came another bang of her arm. "Didi, do you need something? Are you in pain?" Craig asked.

She shook her head no and looked increasingly frustrated.

I said to her, "Mom, I wish I could read your mind. I'm trying, but I just don't understand. We just need to get you off this machine so that we can bring you home to your own bed."

She banged her arm on the bed multiple times and reached for her tube. I knew all that she wanted was to get that tube out of her mouth and to be off the breathing machine. My heart was breaking as I told her that getting the tube out would be a process and we would have to work toward that outcome.

At this point, Craig had moved to the end of the bed to be closer and to comfort me. As if walking out of a room without saying a word, she turned her head to stare into the distance on the other side of the bed. Although I knew what she wanted, I didn't know how to accomplish it. All the facts of reality had set in for me now. She looked exhausted, and it seemed like her body was ready for the fight to be over.

Although we sat with her for a little longer, it seemed like she had disconnected from us now. Praying out loud, I said, "Please, God, please heal her and bring her back to us. Please allow her to breathe off this machine so we can bring her home." I found myself now quietly pleading with God for a miracle. In moments of desperation like this, you think perhaps God will just show his face to answer your prayers, but humbly you realize his answer may be silence.

After Mom slipped into a morphine-induced slumber, we decided it was best to head home for the night. Out in the hall, we stopped by the nurses' station and I said to a nurse, "If only there was a better way to communicate with a patient in my mom's situation. Like an app on a phone or a button on a keyboard that she could push to relay a message when she could no longer write."

Without missing a beat, she looked at me while making direct eye contact and said, "What your mom needs right now is rest so her body can heal."

I realized the nurse failed to understand what I meant, and now I was feeling just as frustrated as Mom probably was.

Day 6

Sunday

Symbolism means very little when life is on the line; one's wishes are the most important thing.

"Today is the day that God made." These words were echoing in my head as my eyes opened for the first time this day. It was November 11, also known as 11-11, and the number had always seemed to have special significance in my world. In my mind, this was the day to decide to take Mom off the life support to let her breathe on her own, if that was even possible now. Almost prophetically, she had never kept it a secret that she didn't want to live on a machine. She told me the answer to a question I never thought I needed an answer to. The crazy part is she did not put me in charge of that decision. Dad was in charge, and he knew her wishes too, but so far, he had made his decisions based on his love for her. It was a difficult position to be in, especially as things seemed bleaker.

Last night, I called and spoke to the night nurse before I went to bed. I asked if they had started to wean her off the machine, but they had not. Based on all the research I had been doing, it said that they should have started that by now, so it concerned me some. After a reassuring conversation, he agreed to start turning down the support to see how she responded. Now it was time to go to the hospital and see.

Upon our arrival, we found out that gowns and gloves were no longer needed while in the room. This came as a bit of a surprise but also a relief since they weren't things of comfort.

The first thing Craig and I noticed when we walked into Mom's room that morning was that her right eye was oddly out of alignment. The only way I can describe what I saw was that it reminded me of a person who had had a stroke that effected the eye. We knew the tumor had spread to her brain, but was this an effect of that or something different? She looked at me in a way that seemed she was in another world; this was sharp contrast to the days prior. Questions began to swirl in my head. If she was taken off life support, what kind of Mom would come home? Would she still be able to color? Would she even know who we were?

While I was pondering these questions and many more, I found out that Mom had pulled the tube out overnight. At that moment, I struggled to understand why they had reintubated her because there was a "Do not resuscitate" order in place. Little did I know the hospital required a "Do not intubate" order as well.

According to the doctors, today was another day of consistency. They phrased her status as "greatly unchanged" when asked. Even though they had reintubated her, the machine was slowly backing off the support and she was maintaining, but not very well. There was an array of numbers to digest, some good and some bad. A nurse, noticing our concern, astutely said, "Don't worry about the numbers. You probably just want to visit with your mom right now."

I knew that was her subtle way of warning that Mom wouldn't be on this earth much longer and we should take the time with her while we could.

I gently wrapped my fingers over top of Mom's hand that was resting on the bed. It was nice to feel my mom's hand in my hand again without a glove between them. Warm to the touch, it still brought me immense comfort in this dull, achy place. If it is possible to have a favorite memory in the ICU, this was mine.

The facts that day were that she wasn't in pain, wasn't progressing well, and doctors were still doing "many interventions" to keep her in sync and alive. One nurse did show me the list of interventions they had to do with her while a second nurse, visibly in awe of the list, confirmed it wasn't a good sign, though not in words as much as in actions. Unlike how I felt in the morning, I was no longer certain what the right decision was for Mom. My father's words came back to me every chance my mind would allow. "It is a process, Amy."

Day 7

Monday

You'll never have all the answers.

Nearly a week had flown by in the blink of an eye. After my normal mom duties, I headed to the hospital alone because Craig had to go back to work. When I arrived to Mom's room, I sat at her side while gospel music played from my Bluetooth speaker. It seemed surreal to be alone with her and to feel so alone at the same time.

Early that morning, a nurse came in to speak with me and requested a "family meeting" to determine next steps. I called Dad and asked when he could come to the hospital to accommodate their request, and he told me he would be there within the hour. He had stopped to make final arrangements for Mom. The doctors had warned yesterday that decisions would need to be made unless there was marked improvement in Mom. They tried their best to educate us about the situation we were facing, but it was hard to understand everything in its entirety. Only yesterday, I felt like I was gently trying to convince my dad of where we were in the process, but now I think I was trying to convince myself. I was starting to understand the details of this process, and they weren't good.

When we met with the doctors and nurses, hospice was quickly introduced into the conversation. It was an option I had not thought about. Dad and I listened to their expert opinions and replied with a few questions. The most poignant was "What are the odds of Mom getting off of this machine and going home?"

According to them, it was not a good prognosis. Of course, none of the doctors would rule out divine intervention, and we hadn't ruled that out either. The hospice nurses, also present at the meeting, were kind and gentle in their responses. It was as if they had the knowledge that came with hundreds of patients before this but the kindest touch to make you feel like this was their first dying mom. This brought a dose of cognitive reality and a resolute chorus that was tasked with helping us ready ourselves to walk the chosen path. Not that we had much of a choice, but the path was becoming clearer with each passing day.

By the end of the meeting, we had come to an arrangement to withdraw the tubes and take Mom off life support in the morning. Ten o'clock sharp was the schedule that would give the nurses the necessary time to go through shift change and check on their newly gained patients. With nods and handshakes, it was cemented.

Day 8

Tuesday

Only God truly knows the plan.

We entered the hospital with what we though would be the plan. Dad, Craig, and I gathered in Mom's room ready for whatever might come next. Clergy stopped in to see if we needed to discuss anything and offer support during this difficult time. The prior week had felt like a movie I was part of but also watching at the same time. Today seemed like the final scenes and all the actors were ready for their parts. Was this really about to happen?

The task of disconnecting Mom from the ventilator was not instantaneous. The nursing staff had gradually decreased the amount of help the machine was offering, but the only way to know if she could breathe on her own would be to completely disconnect her from it. Divine intervention wasn't something you could measure or plan for; only God knew the plan.

Now the doctors came into the room to verify that the decision to disconnect her had not changed. It hadn't. I helplessly sat watching the orchestra of doctors and nurses as they gently removed the tubes from her mouth. When they finished, they removed the restraints that were placed days earlier when she was ripping out her tube and freed her arms.

For the first time in this room since day 1, she looked at peace. I anxiously waited for her to come together, open her eyes, and show life. I selfishly just wanted a hug and acknowledgment that she knew I was with her; most of all, I wanted to hug her without the tubes and restraints. But that moment never came.

She readjusted herself back into the world without the assistance of the machine that she had been relying on to breathe, but she lightly struggled. Although she could get air into her lungs, the doctor suspected that one lung had been overcome with cancer. This, on top of COPD symptoms, meant the air couldn't expand her lungs enough to have a healthy exchange of oxygen for her organs. Being a smoker her entire life minus the last two months had taken away the option of a lung transplant. The test had failed, and we all knew she could not live off the machine. That fact withstanding, she could not live on the machine because it wasn't what Mom wanted.

I hadn't thought of this next part. The doctors gave us all the data leading up to this point. They suggested this is where we would find ourselves based on the science they knew. We never asked what happened if you were right. We just assumed (or at least I did) that they were wrong and when they took that tube out, she would wake up and be ready for a hug. Of course, I knew they had 50 percent chance of being right, to which I would quickly block and return to my hopeful thoughts. Hope is entrancing, it is therapeutic, and it is much kinder than reality.

We knew that putting the tube back in wasn't an option after it had been removed but soon found out that other medical interventions were also now being discontinued. Blood pressure wasn't going to be monitored, cholesterol was not being treated, pulse wasn't a concern, all the machines were turned off, and the room was faded to nearly black. I did not know what the next step was. How could I have missed ever asking that question? Was she in pain? Did her grimacing face from earlier mean she was hurting?

My head raced with thoughts as she just lay there trying to breathe. I stayed by her side, determined to be her strength, *her rock*. I had made a promise after all; I would be there for her last breath. Although I didn't know what that meant, I just knew that it was my duty—my final promise to her.

My heart ached with sadness as I felt my soul floundering in the universe. She was right in front of me, but I missed her so much already. *When would I get to see her again the way I had always known her?*

I leaned over and quietly whispered in her ear, as tears rolled down my face, "I love you so much, Momma! I'm so sorry I couldn't fix this."

As the night came, I had become emotionally drained and exhausted. My perspective on staying changed as I sat by her bedside and thought of my own children. I knew I loved my mom, but no matter what, my kids still needed a mom too. I felt compelled to leave in case she was holding on because I was there in her presence. My knowledge of death was not much more than what you see in the movies, and it seemed logical that she was holding on until I would part.

I made the difficult decision to walk away that night and let God take over.

Day 9

Wednesday

We knew the plan now too.

When I arrived that morning, I got to the ICU to find Mom had been moved. The nurses told me that the room was needed for another critical patient, so they moved her to the eighth floor. Over the past week, we had grown sick of seeing that CAUTI sign, so moving seemed like a nice change.

On my way up to her new room, I could not help but be reminded of a few days prior when I first found Mom had disappeared from her room. The elevator had the same familiar sounds, filled with people I never knew and most likely never will. Some of the other riders wore scrubs and/or exchanged pleasantries while the elevator would pause at each floor to welcome new faces or let some go on their way.

The elevator settled into place at floor 8. When the doors opened, I could see out the picture windows, directly in front of me, sat the majestic view of a grand cathedral—one of the oldest churches in Baltimore. I prayed for strength. Drawing in a deep breath, I closed my eyes with the vision of the old godly church resonating behind my eyelids. I asked for guidance to find peace and love as I was struggling to be on the chosen path.

Amen.

After praying, I opened my eyes and turned a corner in the hall. I found Dad already inside room 828, Mom's new room. Mom's chest still heaved with every raspy breath that met her lungs. Her eyes were shut, her mouth slightly open, and that was how it stayed. She didn't shift positions or move her head; she rested exactly how she was placed. She laid there just breathing in and out. The whole scene seemed very mechanical to me even though the only machine left by her side was the morphine pump.

Everything seemed more somber as Dad and I made conversation that day. As the morning turned to afternoon, we decided to find our way to the cafeteria. It was the first time in days that we had left our guard positions to do something for ourselves, together. It was apparent that her body wasn't getting any better and her situation was not improving.

Divine intervention was what we awaited.

When we returned from lunch, a new nurse had arrived to set up the portable morphine pump so Mom could transition to hospice. She proceeded to set up the pump and ready Mom for transportation in a quick and efficient fashion. Dad had decided he was going to follow the ambulance and get Mom situated in her room at the hospice care center. It was getting late in the day, and I needed to get my children off the bus, so I doled out goodbye hugs and kisses to both Mom and Dad before my departure.

A few hours later, I followed up with Dad to confirm all had gone well. Of course, it had.

Day 10

Thursday

The end was just the beginning.

It had been just one short week from the day she had the biopsy. The week had gone by in the blink of an eye, and it certainly wasn't ending where I thought it would. This was my first time in a hospice center. The building had the appearance of an old-fashioned hospital or nursing home from the outside but seemed quainter on the inside. I entered the softly lit lobby feeling angst as I built up the courage to ask the nurse at the desk where I could find my mother.

The nurse proceeded to escort me to the room, veering off occasionally to point out some amenities and where to find things. "This is the coffee room, and over here is our chapel. If you need the nurse for your mom, you can find her right here," she said.

The walls here were all beige, and the trim was a bright white. The doors, also white, were wooden with stainless door handles that seemed like they were in the shape of a question mark yet curved and smooth. As we walked by rooms to other patients, I could not help but look in a few. Maybe it was my own morbid curiosity or perhaps just trying to better understand what to expect. I'm not sure which.

In the first room, I noticed an older man in the bed with two ladies standing near him. The ladies were dressed in normal, casual attire, and he draped in a hospital gown. One of the ladies looked toward me and we exchanged a wordless question: "Are you here for death too?" In my mind, there was an agreeing nod.

Another room a little farther down, I saw just one person in a bed. No one was next to them. I felt a bit of sadness thinking about how that person might be lonely or possibly die with no one around. "I should go sit with people who are here that don't have anyone," I said to myself. *Perhaps I will do this when Mom has passed,* I thought.

We come to a stop at the second to last door of the hall, and the nurse opened the door. She welcomed me to enter, and there I found Mom.

She appeared ghostly thin and had a white sheet draped from her stomach to her feet with the prayer blanket she had received just a day earlier on top of that. Her breaths were heavy and consistent, the blue hospital gown rising and falling with her every sigh. I saw that her chin was situated in such a way that made it seem as if she was looking off to her side. Her mouth was open, and there was lip moisturizer stationed next to her ear.

The sound of her breaths, coming sharp and fast, were only secondary to the rattling that could be heard in her throat with each consumption of air. Dad, by her side, looked tired and lonely. He smiled when he saw me and began to tell me how the television had a lot of channels. A welcome distraction for him, I guessed, but he had put on Animal Planet, Mom's favorite. After a few pleasantries, he told me he had been here for four hours already. I assured him that if he needed to leave, I had come to sit by her side until I could not sit any longer.

It was about 4:30 p.m. when my dad decided to head home to let the dogs out. I was now alone with Mom again. Inside, I was a mess. I brought a book and my crochet supplies, standards for my entertainment, but at this moment, all I wanted to do was sit there and look at her.

Studying her face, I knew that the time was limited, and I wasn't sure for how much longer I'd get to look at her. I wanted to remember every curve and ridge while I had the opportunity.

Silence overtook the room, and as it did, I felt compelled to do something about it because, throughout Mom's life, it was never quiet like this. I grabbed my phone and typed into the search bar, "Heaven songs." The first song on the search list was one of Mom's favorites! Looking at the title, I mentally flashed back to see Mom standing in our family home's dining room while singing the lyrics and saying how much she loved this song. This was the perfect song, so I hit play.

As the song started, I heard Mom's breathing change. *Can she hear this? Does she like the choice?* I thought. Her breathing slowed down and stopped for a couple of beats. *"Is this it?"* And then she started breathing again. The song continued to a part in the lyrics that said, "I'm gonna walk with my granddaddy." With that line, she took a deep breath in, and as it went out, no more breaths followed.

It was 5:36 p.m.

I sat there for a while longer, listening to a few more songs while I took in the moment. The reality was now looming over me that I would eventually have to get up and make myself move, even though I wasn't sure I wanted to. I knew that whatever spirit was in her body had left her with that last breath. I was truly all alone in that room, sitting in silence.

I called my dad first to tell him the news. He was remorseful that he wasn't here, but I quickly reassured him that if he had been, she wouldn't have let go. "It was her time to go be with her granddaddy, and I know her mom escorted her too," I said.

After that, Michael called, and he was the one who ultimately got me to move. He said, "Amy, why are you just sitting there? That's creepy. Don't sit there too long." It was good advice and the permission I felt like I needed to leave.

I hung up the phone and stepped out toward the nurses' station. I barely had to say the words; they either saw them on my face or could read my mind.

We went back in the room, where they verified my words and noted the official time of death. I gathered my things from the room, kissed Mom on her head, and said one final goodbye officially.

Just Because I Love You

I thought of you this morning,
As I looked out at the view,
So, I said a little prayer,
"Just because I love you."

I asked God to watch over
Everything you say and do,
And bless each step you would take,
"Just because I love you."

Then I went about my day,
Oh, how the hours flew.
Then at bedtime, again I prayed,
"Just because I love you."

I asked the Lord to keep you safe,
All the long night thru.
Quickly He replied, "I will",
"Just because I love you."

by Shirley Leech

Printed in the United States
by Baker & Taylor Publisher Services